Adjectives and Adverbs

Kara Murray

PowerKiDS press™

New York

Published in 2014 by The Rosen Publishing Group, Inc.
29 East 21st Street, New York, NY 10010

First Edition

Editor: Amelie von Zumbusch
Book Design: Colleen Bialecki

Photo Credits: Cover Mel Yates/Taxi/Getty Images; p. 5 Mieke Dalle/Photographer's Choice RF/ Getty Images; p. 6 Holbox/Shutterstock.com; p. 7 Alfredo Maiquez/Shutterstock.com; p. 8 nbiebach/ Shutterstock.com; p. 9 Catalin Petolea/Shutterstock.com; p. 11 Monkey Business Images/Shutterstock.com; p. 13 Polka Dot Images/Thinkstock; p. 14 Image Source/Getty Images; p. 15 Creatas/Thinkstock.com; p. 17 Wealan Pollard/Ojo Images/Getty Images; p. 18 Laura Fasulo/Flickr/Getty Images; p. 19 Rainer Elstermann/Litesize/Thinkstock; p. 21 Jon Feingersh/Blend images/Getty images.

Library of Congress Cataloging-in-Publication Data
Murray, Kara.
  Adjectives and adverbs / by Kara Murray. – First edition.
    pages cm. — (Core Language Skills)
  Includes index.
  ISBN 978-1-4777-0799-9 (library binding) — ISBN 978-1-4777-0970-2 (pbk.) —
  ISBN 978-1-4777-0971-9 (6-pack)
  1. English language—Adjective—Juvenile literature. 2. English language—Adverb—Juvenile literature.
  3. English language—Grammar—Juvenile literature. I. Title.
  PE1241.M87 2014
  428.2—dc23
                              2012045401
Manufactured in the United States of America

CPSIA Compliance Information: Batch #S13PK5: For Further Information contact Rosen Publishing, New York, New York at 1-800-237-9932

Contents

Describing Words

What are the words that add spice to our sentences? They are **adjectives** and **adverbs**! Adjectives are words that describe **nouns**. Adverbs describe **verbs**. A noun is a person, place, or thing. Many nouns are things that we can touch, see, smell, or feel. A verb is an action word. Verbs are actions that nouns can take.

A sentence without either adjectives or adverbs can give you information, but it will not tell you much. For example, compare these two sentences:

The dog runs.

The black dog runs fast.

Which sentence gives you a better picture in your mind?

What adjectives would you use to describe this boy? What adverbs could describe how he is picking out candy?

(See answers on p. 22)

FIGURE IT OUT

Can you identify the adjectives and adverbs in the following sentence?

Sara quickly grabbed the comfortable chair.

Different Kinds of Adjectives

Adjectives supply many ways to describe how something look, feels, tastes, or acts. Did you know that numbers can be adjectives? They tell us how many of a noun is being talked about. Colors can be adjectives, too.

You may be wondering how to pick which adjectives to use. It helps to think about exactly what you want to say.

What adjectives would you use to describe the girl on the left? How about the girl on the right?

This is a crimson-backed tanager. Crimson is a particular shade of red. Picking adjectives that describe things exactly helps others picture those things more clearly.

Look at these three sentences:
My brother is happy.
My brother is pleased.
My brother is joyful.
Each one says something slightly different. To pick the best adjective, think hard about what you want to tell your reader about your brother's feelings.

FIGURE IT OUT

The adjectives "enraged," "displeased," and "angry" have related, but different, meanings. Can you list them from least upset to most upset?

(See answers on p. 22)

7

Noun, Verb, or Adjective?

Did you know that nouns are sometimes used as adjectives? Colors are words that can be both. "Blue" is a noun in the sentence "Blue is my favorite color." It is an adjective in the sentence "I wore my blue shirt." It describes the noun "shirt."

A "sitting duck" means a duck that is not flying. In this term, "sitting" is used as an adjective. It describes the duck.

This boy is in an apple orchard. In the term "apple orchard," the noun "apple" acts as an adjective. It tells you what kind of orchard is being described.

Do you know what kinds of words end in "ing" or "ed"? If you said verbs, you are right! However, verbs that end in "ing," "ed," or "en," can also act as adjectives. For example, "waiting" is an adjective in the sentence "There is a waiting list to join this class." It describes the list.

FIGURE IT OUT

Can you pick out the verb and adjective in this sentence?

We gave our completed project to the teacher.

(See answers on p. 22)

All About Adverbs

Just like adjectives, adverbs are words used to describe. Adverbs, though, are used to describe verbs, other adverbs, adjectives, and **phrases**.

If you wanted to write about how a monkey climbs up a tree, how might you describe it? You could write that it climbs easily. "Easily" is an adverb that tells us how the monkey climbs. You might also write that it climbs very easily. In this case, "very" and "easily" are both adverbs. "Very" is describing "easily."

Adverbs tell us how, when, where, why, or how often something happens. They tell us so much about how things are done!

These kids are smiling happily. Can you think of any other adverbs that would describe the way they are smiling?

FIGURE IT OUT

Can you find the adverbs in this sentence?

Gabe hit the ground hard and badly scraped his knee.

(See answers on p. 22)

Adverb Clues

There is a clue that helps you guess that a word might be an adverb. Many adverbs end in "ly." When you add "ly" to an adjective, you make an adverb! Think about how you did your homework last night. You could have done it "carefully," "correctly," "easily," or "quietly."

Making Adverbs from Adjectives

Adjective	sudden	recent	common	loud
Adverb	suddenly	recently	commonly	loudly

These girls are running quickly. If you wanted to use a different adjective, you could say that they are running speedily or rapidly.

When writing, remember that adverbs help paint a clearer picture in a reader's mind. If you are writing about a trip you took, think about how it went. Did you arrive quickly or did it take a long time to get there? What adverbs could you use to describe how you traveled?

FIGURE IT OUT

How would you make adverbs out of the following adjectives?

Beautiful
Clever
Amazing

(See answers on p. 22)

The Other Adverbs

While most adverbs are formed by adding "ly" to adjectives, a few are not. "Late," "fast," and "hard" do not take an "ly" when they become adverbs. The adjective "good" becomes the adverb "well." You just have to remember these adverbs.

Certain adverbs are used to tell us how much, or to what **degree**, something is true. One of these is "very."

It is correct to say that someone "played well," rather than that they "played good." Since you want to describe the verb "played," use the form that is an adverb.

Many of the adverbs that describe how actions are timed do not end in "ly." These include "late," "never," "always," and "sometimes."

If you write "I walked very softly through the house," that is a little different from writing "I walked softly through the house." Both describe the same action, but the first brings attention to just how softly you walked.

FIGURE IT OUT

Can you use "very" to change the degree of the adverbs in the following sentences?

Jake ran slowly to first base.

Maria happily announced that she could come to my birthday party.

(See answers on p. 22)

Where Do They Go?

You might be wondering where in a sentence to put adjectives and adverbs. Adjectives often go right in front of the nouns they are describing. Let's say you want to describe a boy's visit to a doctor. You want to note that the doctor is tall and the boy is sick. You would write, "The sick boy visited the tall doctor."

When adverbs are describing verbs, they usually follow the verbs. If you want to write that someone was quiet while sitting, you would write that she sat quietly. When adverbs are used to describe adjectives, they should come before the adjectives.

"Late" is an adverb in the sentence "I was late for school." It goes after the verb "was." It is an adjective in "There were two late students." There, it goes before the noun "students."

Is the word order in the following sentences correct?

The big, black dog is mine.

The tended carefully roses were beautiful.

(See answers on p. 22)

Discovering New Words

You can often find the meaning of unfamiliar adjectives or adverbs by looking at their **context**. Let's say you read the sentences: "I am very full. That sandwich I ate was enormous." Since eating that sandwich made the speaker so full, you might guess that "enormous" means "very big."

Endings called suffixes offer clues to a word's meaning, too. For example, some adjectives end in the suffix "ful." As you might guess, "peaceful" means "full of peace."

Try to guess what "excessively" means from this sentence: "The jackhammer's excessively loud noise gave me a big headache."

Another way to figure out a word's meaning is to look at its root. Say you come across the unfamiliar word "dishonestly." Its **root** is "honest." The **prefix** "dis" at the beginning of a word reverses that word's meaning. You can guess that "dishonestly" means "in a way that is not honest."

FIGURE IT OUT

Can you use roots and context to figure out what the italicized words mean?

My mom said to stay away from that dog because it is *unfriendly*.

I had been scared to get a flu shot, but it was *painless*.

(See answers on p. 22)

19

Look It Up!

You can't always figure out a word's meaning from its context or root words. Sometimes, you have to look it up in a **dictionary**. Dictionaries tell you what words mean and how to **pronounce** them. They list words alphabetically. A dictionary is a useful tool to keep nearby when reading.

Some books, like this one, have **glossaries** in the back. A glossary is like a dictionary just for that book. **Thesauruses** are handy for writing. They list words with related or opposite meanings.

It would be hard to describe things without adjectives and adverbs. They make our language much more interesting!

Dictionaries can tell you the meanings of thousands of different words!

FIGURE IT OUT

Can you use a dictionary to find out what "beloved" means? Does it come before or after the word "believe" in the dictionary?

(See answers on p. 22)

Figure It Out: The Answers

Page 5: "Quickly" is an adverb describing "grabbed," and "comfortable" is an adjective describing "chair."

Page 7: "Displeased" is the least upset, "angry" is in the middle, and "enraged" is the most upset.

Page 9: "Gave" is the verb, and "completed" is the adjective.

Page 11: "Hard" and "badly" are both adverbs.

Page 13: "Beautiful" becomes the adverb "beautifully." "Clever" becomes "cleverly." "Amazing" becomes the adverb "amazingly."

Page 15: The first sentence should read, "Jake ran very slowly to first base." The second should say, "Maria very happily announced that she could come to my birthday party."

Page 17: The first sentence is correct. The second one is not. It should read, "The carefully tended roses were beautiful."

Page 19: The word "unfriendly" means "not kind or pleasant." The word "painless" means "without pain."

Page 21: "Beloved" means "very much loved." It comes after "believe." Since the words have the same first three letters, you look at the fourth letter to see which comes first. "Beloved" comes after "believe" because "o" comes after "i" in the alphabet.

adjectives (A-jik-tivs) Words that describe something.

adverbs (AD-verbz) Words that describe actions, adjectives, or other adverbs.

context (KON-tekst) Words around a word that make that word's meaning clearer.

degree (dih-GREE) The amount, level, or reach of something.

dictionary (DIK-shuh-ner-ee) A book that lists words alphabetically and explains their meanings.

glossaries (GLAH-suh-reez) Alphabetical lists of words and their meanings.

nouns (NOWNZ) A person, place, idea, state, or thing.

phrases (FRAYZ-ez) Groups of words that have meaning but are missing subjects or verbs.

prefix (PREE-fiks) A group of letters that comes at the beginning of a word and that has a meaning of its own.

pronounce (pruh-NOWNS) To make the sounds of words.

root (ROOT) The base part of a word.

thesauruses (thih-SOR-us-ez) Books that list words that are alike and words that are different from each other.

verbs (VERBZ) Words that describe actions.

Index

Websites

Due to the changing nature of Internet links, PowerKids Press has developed an online list of websites related to the subject of this book. This site is updated regularly. Please use this link to access the list:

www.powerkidslinks.com/cls/adj/